Dribbles

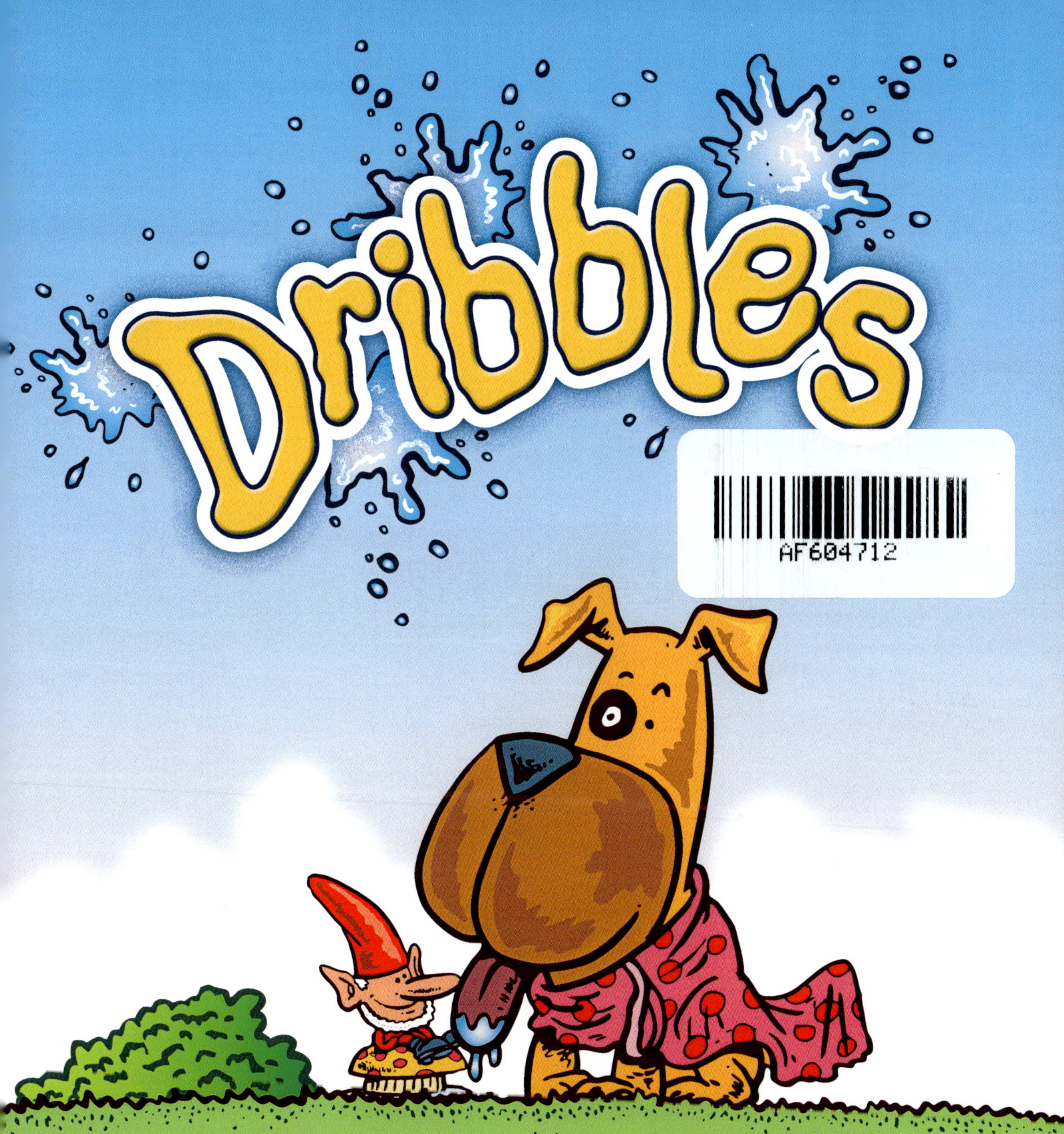

A play by Michael Wagner

Illustrated by Martin Chatterton

Characters

Tom

Lulu

Trixie
(a friend)

Mum
Gnome
Dribbles

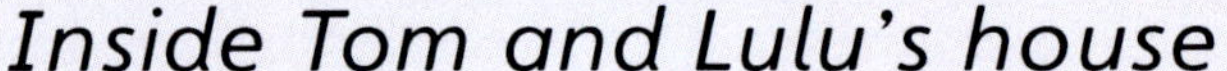

Inside Tom and Lulu's house

Mum: Tom! Lulu! Come here, right now!

Tom: What, Mum?

Lulu: Have we been naughty?

Mum: No ... not yet. I just need you to do **one** small job.

Tom: We love small jobs.

Lulu: The smaller the better.

Mum: We're going to Anna's party in ten minutes. I just have to pick up a cake from the shop over the road.

Mum: Your job is to get into your fancy dress costumes before I get back. Can you do that?

Tom: Sure, Mum.

Lulu: That's easy!

Mum: Great. Now, your costumes are out in the backyard on the clothes line. I'll be back in ten minutes. Please be ready to go.

Tom: Where did you say our costumes are?

Mum: They're on the clothes line. Got to go! I will be back soon.

Mum exits.

Lulu: Let's get our costumes, Tom.

Tom: You know who's out in the backyard, don't you?

Lulu: Who?

Tom: He's big. He's got four legs and he licks everyone all over!

Lulu: Dribbles!

Dribbles: WOOF! WOOF!

Lulu: Oh no! Dribbles licks your face. He licks your ears. He even licks inside your nose! How can we get our costumes without getting licked, Tom?

Tom: I've got a plan.

Lulu: You're the best big brother ever!

Tom: Come on. We need to go around to Trixie's house.

In Trixie's backyard

Tom: Thanks for lending us your ladder, Trixie.

Trixie: You're welcome! But why is there a dog in your backyard?

Lulu: That's Gran's dog, Dribbles. We're looking after him while Gran's away.

Trixie: He looks very friendly.

Tom: That's the problem, Trixie. He's **too** friendly!

Over the fence in Tom and Lulu's backyard

Dribbles: Woof, woof! Pant, pant! Slurp, slurp!

Gnome: Stop licking my ear!

Dribbles: Ears are good. Lick, lick! Slobber, slobber!

Gnome: Yuck! Stop licking me, Dribbles! I don't need a bath.

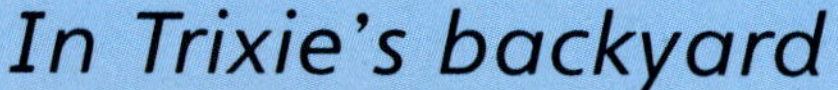

In Trixie's backyard

Tom: Can you help us with the ladder, Trixie?

Trixie: Yes, but what are you doing with it?

Lulu: We're making a bridge from the top of your fence to the top of the clothes line. It's Tom's plan.

Tom: Then we can get our costumes without getting licked.

Lulu: We don't like Dribbles' slobber.

Trixie: That's not a good plan.

Tom: It's a great plan.

They lift the ladder into place.

Trixie: I'll get you some helmets.

Tom: Look, Trixie! Lulu and I are on the ladder and Dribbles can't reach us.

Lulu: Dribbles can't lick us up here!

Trixie: It's still a bad plan. I just know it.

Dribbles: If I jump a little higher, I might reach Tom's leg! Arf! Arf arf!

Gnome: Give up, Dribbles. They're too high.

Dribbles: Must … lick … legs! Woof, woof!

Gnome: Forget it, Dribbles! Let them get their costumes.

Dribbles: Whine, whine.

Dribbles jumps higher and gets tangled in Mum's dress.

Gnome: Get your head out of that dress, Dribbles!

Dribbles: I'm stuck! Growl, growl!

Dribbles panics and starts running.

Trixie: Stop running, Dribbles! You're making the clothes line spin!

Dribbles: Help! YELP!

Lulu: The ladder is wobbling, Tom!

Tom: Quick, Lulu, jump down and grab your costume. Then run inside.

Lulu: Tom, I can't hold on!

Tom: Neither can I!

Tom:
Lulu: AAHHHH!

Trixie: See? I knew it was a bad plan.

Mum enters the backyard.

Trixie: Here comes your mum! See you later.

Mum: I'm back, Tom and Lulu, and I gave you one small job! I bet you haven't done it ... Oh, you have! Wow!

Lulu: Yes! Look, Mum!

Tom: We got into our costumes just like you asked us to.

Lulu: We're even ready to go!

Tom: Well, just as soon as you get us off the clothes line.

Mum: (*laughing*) It was clever of you to dress up Dribbles. He can come to the party too.

Dribbles: I'm going to a party! Yes! Lick, lick! Slobber, slobber! Slurp, slurp!

Tom:
Lulu: NOOOOOOO!

Trixie: I knew it was a bad plan.

Gnome: It looks like Trixie was right.